Intentionally Positive

Live to inspire the next
generation.

Paperback ISBN: 978-1-953364-40-1

Infinite Generations
137 National Plaza, STE 300
National Harbor, MD 20745

Printed in the United States of America

First Printing, 2023

Art by Canva
Cover Design by: I Howard

Positive Media, Happy Life

www.InfiniteGenerations.com

Intentionally Positive

Taking the time to put you first.

– Shani T. Night

Dear Reader:

Thank you for your purchase.
I hope you enjoy Intentionally Positive.

Please share a review of this book on Amazon.

Visit my website for more content, discounts, contests, giveaways,
and/or a free consult.
www.shanitnight.com

Follow Shani Night:
instagram.com/shaninight
www.facebook.com/ShaniTNight
I post daily/weekly positive messages.

WHEN YOU FOCUS ON THE GOOD, THE GOOD GETS BETTER.

Intentionally Positive

Intentionally Positive is a mindset that focuses on choosing positive thoughts, actions, and behaviors in order to create a more fulfilling and purposeful life. It involves being mindful and intentional in our approach to life, and actively seeking out opportunities for growth, happiness, and fulfillment.

An intentionally positive person is someone who takes responsibility for their own happiness and well-being and approaches life with a sense of optimism and hope. They cultivate a positive mindset by focusing on what is good in their life, practicing gratitude, and setting goals that align with their values and vision for the future.

Stop here if you purchased this book before completing Vol. I.
You will need Vol. I before you can understand what we're doing in Vol. II. Reach out to me for a discount for Vol. I.

Intentionally Positive coaching helps individuals cultivate this mindset and develop strategies for integrating it into their daily lives. Through coaching sessions, clients learn to identify negative patterns of thinking and behavior and replace them with positive alternatives. They also learn how to set goals and take action in order to create a more fulfilling and purposeful life.

Intentionally Positive coaching can benefit individuals in a variety of contexts, including personal relationships, career development, and overall well-being. It is a powerful tool for overcoming self-doubt, cultivating resilience, and finding a sense of purpose and direction in life.

WWW.SHANITNIGHT.COM

IT'S ABOUT LIFE-
CHANGING MOVES. SO
TAKE THE FIRST STEP IN
THE RIGHT DIRECTION
TODAY!

Intentionally Positive

Intentionally Positive is a mindset that focuses on choosing positive thoughts, actions, and behaviors in order to create a more fulfilling and purposeful life. It involves being mindful and intentional in our approach to life, and actively seeking out opportunities for growth, happiness, and fulfillment.

What I ask of you:

- Keep an open mind. Be willing to use the tool of introspection, as it allows individuals to examine their inner world and make adjustments to their thoughts and behaviors as necessary.
- Be willing to learn. Become a student of your own life.
- Be curious about your feelings and your reactions. Willing to investigate to find your truth.
- Be motivated to change and willing to accept those changes.
- Be willing to do the work. Guided 1-minute activities for your journey along with fun exercises to explore mindfulness.
- Follow through on commitments. Be persistent. Be consistent. Be intentional.
- Take the initiative to carry forward what you take away from each lesson into your daily life.
- **Do not rush through the book.**
- Incorporate mindfulness into your daily routine, whether you are a beginner or an experienced practitioner. We can explore a low-stress approach tailored to your needs, or build upon your existing skills to enhance your practice.

I LOVE QUOTES BECAUSE
THEY ARE THE
SHORTENED EXPRESSION
OF ALL OF THE
EMOTIONS ONE IS
FEELING.

Shani T. Night

H.U.G.S

H.U.G.S is a four-step process I created for dealing with negativity and healing my mind to stay positive. As you go through the process of introspection it can be challenging but by using this process below, you will empower yourself to heal and stay positive, comfort and strengthen yourself by using the inner strength you naturally harness.

I know of one other tool that works so easily and quickly, but when my clients are done and compare the two tools, H.U.G.S is the most selected. My clients have told me the process is quick, comforting, and immediately rewarding. When done consistently, it's life-changing in the process of being intentionally positive.

Step 1 - H
HUG yourself to provide the comfort and courage you need to heal. Preferably forearms or where you can feel skin.

Step 2- U
Use your inner intuition, power, and strength for a resurgence of the strength and power you harness from within.
Think of all your strengths and use them in thought to build on strengthening.

STEP 3 - G
Give yourself a positive boost with positive words.
Remember 3 positive affirmations you can tell yourself daily to give you the positive encouragement you need.

Think positive thoughts.

STEP 4 - S
Strength is now within you to release and move forward.

HEAL, USE, GIVE, STRENGTH (H.U.G.S.)

A Good Day Starts with Positivity and Sunshine!

Shani T. Night

Good Morning Sunshine

(I always welcome sunshine into my day, first thing in the morning: so welcome sunshine and an open heart to declutter your mind. Continue to do this each day. Share thoughts on how you feel about doing this below.)

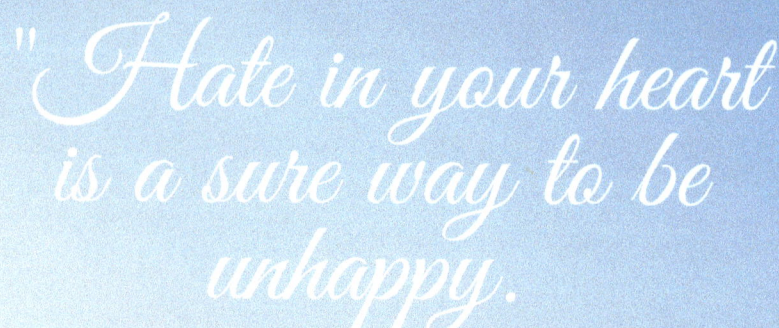

"Hate in your heart is a sure way to be unhappy.

Joy is better. Let joy in today!"

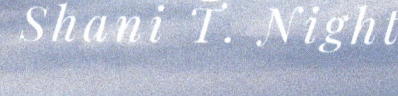

Shani T. Night

Good Morning Sunshine

(I always welcome sunshine into my day, first thing in the morning: so welcome sunshine and an open heart to declutter your mind. Now let's add something new to your morning. List 3 things you are grateful for today. Continue to do this each day.)

THE KEY IS TO START INCLUDING BEHAVIORS THAT WILL IMPROVE YOUR SENSE OF WELL-BEING. CONSISTENT PRACTICES CREATE NEW HABITS.

Morning Vision

(We started in Vol. I (Book 1) creating a morning routine. Now let's add to it.

Add a few more positive steps to your morning. Pick one of the below exercises.)

Create reminders of joy around you. Visual reminders can increase positive feelings.

Write affirmations on your bathroom mirror
We spend a lot of time in our bathrooms, washing our hands, brushing our teeth, and so on. Write on the mirror affirmations or positive messages.

Affirmation cards
Affirmation cards are small cards with positive affirmations or inspiring quotes written on them. You can keep them in your wallet, on your desk, or in your car as a reminder to stay positive and focused on your goals.

Post-it notes
You can write positive affirmations or motivational quotes on post-it notes and place them around your home or workspace. They can serve as gentle reminders to stay positive and focused throughout the day.

Create a vision board
Vision boards can be powerful not only in taking the time to create one, but also there is power in looking at it on a regular basis and reminding yourself what is important to you right now.

A vision board is a collage of images and words that represent your goals, dreams, and aspirations. It can serve as a visual reminder of what you want to achieve and help you stay motivated towards your goals.

Inspirational posters
Inspirational posters with uplifting quotes or images can serve as a positive visual reminder to stay motivated and focused on your goals. You can hang them in your office, bedroom, or anywhere else you spend a lot of time.

THE KEY IS TO START INCLUDING BEHAVIORS THAT WILL IMPROVE YOUR SENSE OF WELL-BEING. CONSISTENT PRACTICES CREATE NEW HABITS.

Intentionally Positive

THE KEY IS TO START INCLUDING BEHAVIORS THAT WILL IMPROVE YOUR SENSE OF WELL-BEING. CONSISTENT PRACTICES CREATE NEW HABITS.

Intentionally Positive

(Now add something just for you that you can do every morning. I added a morning and evening skin routine that I look forward to each day. It has a positive impact on my days and nights.)

THE KEY IS TO START INCLUDING BEHAVIORS THAT WILL IMPROVE YOUR SENSE OF WELL-BEING. CONSISTENT PRACTICES CREATE NEW HABITS.

Intentionally Positive

Clear your path to greatness

Shani T. Night

Intentionally Positive

THE KEY IS TO START INCLUDING BEHAVIORS THAT WILL IMPROVE YOUR SENSE OF WELL-BEING. CONSISTENT PRACTICES CREATE NEW HABITS.

Ecotherapy

Ecotherapy is a form of therapy that involves connecting with nature as a way of improving mental health and well-being. It involves engaging in outdoor activities, such as gardening, hiking, or nature walks, as well as practicing mindfulness and meditation in natural settings.

The idea behind ecotherapy is that connecting with nature can have a positive impact on our mental health and well-being. Spending time in natural environments can reduce stress, improve mood, and increase feelings of relaxation and happiness. It can also help us feel more connected to the natural world and to others, which can improve our overall sense of well-being.

Ecotherapy can be practiced in many different ways, from simply spending time in nature to participating in organized nature-based programs. Some ecotherapy programs may involve group activities, such as wilderness retreats or outdoor adventure programs, while others may focus on individual activities, such as gardening or birdwatching.

Overall, ecotherapy is a holistic approach to improving mental health and well-being by incorporating the healing power of nature into our daily lives. It is a growing field that offers a variety of approaches and techniques for connecting with the natural world and improving our mental and emotional health.

Ecotherapy

(Pick one exercise from below and be intentional about it. No distractions, don't rush it, be fully aware of the sights, sounds, and smells around you, take some time to breathe, and be safe. You don't have to always find a forest, as long as there is green in your visual space.)

Here are a few ecotherapy exercises that can help you connect with nature and improve your mental and emotional well-being:

Nature walk
Take a slow, mindful walk through a park, forest, or other natural environments. Use your senses to take in the sights, sounds, and smells of the natural surroundings.

Gardening
Engage in gardening activities, such as planting, watering, and weeding. Connect with the soil, plants, and natural environment around you.

Forest bathing
Spend time in a forest or natural environment, taking in the atmosphere and surroundings. Focus on being present in the moment and engaging with the natural world around you.

Outdoor yoga or meditation
Practice yoga or meditation in a natural environment, such as a park or garden. Connect with the natural surroundings and use them to help deepen your practice.

Birdwatching
Spend time observing and identifying different bird species in a natural environment. Connect with the natural world around you and learn more about the local ecosystem.

Beach therapy
Spend time on the beach, connecting with the sounds and rhythms of the ocean. Walk along the shoreline, collect shells, or simply sit and watch the waves.

Nature photography
Use photography as a way to connect with nature and capture the beauty of the natural world around you. Explore different natural environments and use your camera to capture the unique features of each location.

Overall, ecotherapy exercises are about engaging with the natural world in a mindful, intentional way. These exercises can help reduce stress, improve mood, and promote overall health and well-being.

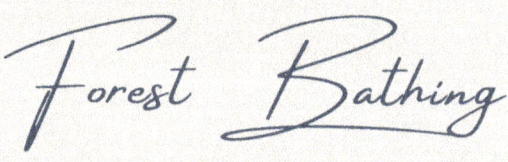

Forest Bathing

Forest bathing, also known as Shinrin-yoku, is a Japanese practice of immersing oneself in nature and taking in the atmosphere of the forest to promote health and well-being. The practice involves slowly and mindfully walking through a forest or natural environment, taking in the sights, sounds, and smells of the natural surroundings.

The concept behind forest bathing is based on the idea that exposure to nature can have a positive impact on our physical and mental health. Studies have shown that spending time in nature can reduce stress, improve mood, boost the immune system, and lower blood pressure and heart rate.

Forest bathing is not about physical exercise or hiking, but rather about being present in the natural environment and connecting with nature. It involves slowing down, engaging the senses, and being mindful of the natural surroundings. This can include activities such as taking deep breaths of fresh air, listening to the sound of the wind or birds, feeling the texture of tree bark, or observing the way sunlight filters through the leaves.

In many countries, forest bathing is recognized as a form of therapy and is often offered as a treatment for stress-related illnesses. It is also becoming more popular as a way to promote mental and physical health and well-being. Overall, forest bathing is a simple and enjoyable way to reduce stress, improve mood, and connect with nature.

Intentionally Positive

THE KEY IS TO START INCLUDING BEHAVIORS THAT WILL IMPROVE YOUR SENSE OF WELL-BEING. CONSISTENT PRACTICES CREATE NEW HABITS.

"

WHEN YOU FOCUS
ON THE GOOD,
THE GOOD GETS
BETTER.

Reflect

(Now that you've completed a few different exercises, how do you feel about the work you've put in? Which exercises had the greatest impact and why? Can you do this exercise more often or on a regular basis?)

_____
_____
_____
_____
_____
_____
_____
_____
_____
_____
_____
_____
_____
_____
_____

Positive vs Negative

Positive and negative are two opposite concepts that can be applied to various aspects of life, including emotions, behaviors, thoughts, and attitudes. Positivity usually refers to a constructive and optimistic outlook towards life, characterized by emotions like joy, gratitude, contentment, and hope. Positive behaviors and attitudes can help individuals build resilience, cope with challenges, and achieve their goals.

On the other hand, negativity often refers to a pessimistic or cynical attitude towards life, characterized by emotions like anger, frustration, sadness, and anxiety. Negative behaviors and attitudes can limit individuals' potential, cause stress and conflict, and hinder their ability to achieve their goals.

It is important to note that positivity and negativity are not fixed traits, but rather a state of mind that can be developed and nurtured through various practices and habits. Cultivating positivity can lead to greater life satisfaction, better mental and physical health, and stronger social connections, while reducing negativity can lead to a greater sense of peace and well-being.

Reflect

(Now that you know more about the impact of negative vs. positive, reflect on what you've learned and how your negative thoughts impact your life.
Next, reflect on your positive thoughts and how they impact your life. For every negative thought you have today and the next, counter it with a positive affirmation from your previous exercise or write a new one down.)

_____
_____
_____
_____
_____
_____
_____
_____
_____
_____
_____
_____
_____
_____

There's something about consistency

Shani T. Night

Consistency

Consistency refers to the quality of being constant or steadfast in behavior, adherence to principles, or performance. It involves showing up regularly and maintaining a standard of excellence in what one does. Consistency is an important characteristic for achieving success in many areas of life, such as work, personal development, relationships, and health. It requires discipline, focus, and dedication to maintain consistency, even in the face of challenges and obstacles. Consistency helps build trust, credibility, and reliability, and it can lead to greater satisfaction and achievement over time.

Consistent practices can create new habits. Habits are behaviors that become automatic through repetition and practice, and consistent practice is the key to forming new habits. When we engage in a behavior consistently over a period of time, our brains start to develop neural pathways that make that behavior more automatic and ingrained. Eventually, the behavior becomes a habit, and we no longer have to consciously think about it or put effort into doing it. For example, if we consistently practice positive thinking every morning, over time it will become a habit and we will no longer have to think about it or force ourselves to think that way. It will simply become a natural part of our daily routine.

However, forming new habits can be challenging, and it requires discipline and commitment to stick to a consistent practice until it becomes a habit. It's important to choose practices that align with our values and goals and to make a conscious effort to practice them consistently over time.

So, if you want to create new habits, consistent practice is a great place to start. By making small, positive changes every day and sticking to them over time, you can form new habits that will help you achieve your goals and improve your life.

"Growth and evolution are not regarded the same because everyone does not evolve at the same time."
-Shan T. Night

We Need More Compassion!
We Need Understanding!
We Need Love!

Consistency

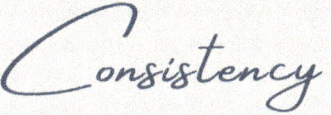

Consistent positive practice creates progress and growth. When we consistently engage in positive practices, such as exercise, meditation, or learning new skills, we create positive habits that can lead to long-term growth and development.

By making positive practices a regular part of our lives, we can build momentum toward our goals and make steady progress over time. Consistency is key, as it allows us to reap the benefits of our positive practices and make them a permanent part of our daily routines.

Consistent positive practice can also help us overcome obstacles and setbacks. By focusing on the progress we have made, rather than on the challenges we face, we can stay motivated and continue to move forward toward our goals.

Overall, consistent positive practice is an essential ingredient for personal growth and development. By making small, positive changes every day, we can create a better future for ourselves and for those around us.

There's something about patience.

Shani T. Night

Patience

Patience is the capacity to remain calm and composed in the face of adversity, uncertainty, or difficult circumstances. Patience is often seen as a virtue, as it can help us maintain a sense of perspective and avoid overreacting or making hasty decisions.

Patience enables us to better understand and empathize with others, as we take the time to listen and communicate effectively.

This is a skill we all need to navigate life's challenges with greater resilience and equanimity.

Keep your mind clear and your heart at peace.   I read somewhere that calmness is a superpower. If so, it's a superpower we all want and need.

Be willing to accept the slowness of change.

Shani T. Night

 Change

Life's challenges require us to be flexible with ourselves. "Be willing to accept the slowness of change" means that meaningful and lasting change takes time and effort. It is often tempting to seek quick fixes or instant gratification, but real change requires patience, persistence, and a willingness to embrace the process.

When we embark on a journey of personal growth or change, we may encounter obstacles, setbacks, and moments of doubt. We may not see immediate results or feel a sense of progress. However, it is important to recognize that change is a gradual process that unfolds over time.

Being willing to accept the slowness of change means having the patience and perseverance to stay the course, even when it feels difficult or frustrating. It means focusing on small, incremental steps and celebrating progress along the way, rather than fixating on the end goal.

Ultimately, being willing to accept the slowness of change means being committed to the journey, rather than just the destination. It means recognizing that meaningful change takes time and effort, and being willing to embrace the process with openness, curiosity, and resilience.

"Time is patience, and patience is living. Living is free."

Shani T. Night

Reflect

(Now that you know more about patience, consistency, and change, think about how you can apply them to your life?)

_____
_____
_____
_____
_____
_____
_____
_____
_____
_____
_____
_____
_____
_____
_____

THE KEY IS TO START INCLUDING BEHAVIORS THAT WILL IMPROVE YOUR SENSE OF WELL-BEING. CONSISTENT PRACTICES CREATE NEW HABITS.

"Have hope in the future, trust in your dreams, and love for what you do. So keep going, keep trusting in yourself, and keep love in your heart."

Shani T. Night

Mood Boosters

(Add mood boosters for stressful days.)

Create one of the following and use it:

- A go-to movie list that either makes you happy, makes you laugh, or that makes you feel all your emotions. Feeling all of your emotions is not a bad thing, sometimes you have to get it all out.

- If you're not a movie person, go for a good book that has the same impact. One that you can re-read over and over.

- If you're not either of the above, create a music playlist for all your moods (one for anger, one for sadness, one for happiness, One for love, one for confidence)

- Last but not least, a good podcast might work. Pick a podcast that inspires you or motivates you. Check out my intentionally positive podcasts for some inspirational listening.

THE KEY IS TO HAVE THE TOOLS TO FEEL THE ENTIRE SPECTRUM OF EMOTIONS. GET CONNECTED WITH ALL OF YOUR FEELING SO YOU CAN EXPERIENCE JOY MORE FULLY.

"

#SELFLOVE IS THE BEST LOVE SO LOVE YOURSELF FIRST, AND THE REST WILL FOLLOW...

Intentionally Positive

(Take a self-love day. Do what you love and what feels good.)

A self-love day is a dedicated day for focusing on and taking care of yourself, both physically and emotionally. It is a day to prioritize your own well-being and practice self-care.

A self-love day may include a variety of activities, depending on your personal preferences and needs.

Here are some examples:

1. Taking a relaxing bath or shower
2. Doing a face mask or other pampering skincare routine
3. Practicing yoga or meditation
4. Going for a walk or doing some other form of exercise
5. Eating nourishing and healthy foods
6. Spending time in nature
7. Reading a book or listening to music
8. Writing in a journal or practicing gratitude
9. Doing something creative, like painting or drawing
10. Spending time with loved ones who uplift and support you.

Remember, self-love is a daily practice, and taking a dedicated self-love day can be a powerful way to nurture your mind, body, and soul.

Self-love and self-care are different concepts, although they are often used interchangeably.

Self-love refers to accepting and appreciating oneself for who they are, flaws and all. It involves recognizing your own worth and treating yourself with kindness, respect, and compassion. Self-love is about developing a positive and nurturing relationship with yourself and prioritizing your own well-being.

On the other hand, self-care refers to intentional actions and practices that you take to improve your physical, emotional, and mental health. Self-care activities can include exercise, healthy eating, getting enough rest, spending time with loved ones, pursuing hobbies, or engaging in activities you enjoy.

While self-care can be an expression of self-love, it is not a substitute for it. Self-love is an underlying belief and attitude towards oneself, while self-care is a set of practices and actions.

THE KEY IS TO INTENTIONALLY SET ASIDE TIME FOR YOURSELF AND ENGAGE IN ACTIVITIES THAT HELP YOU FEEL GOOD, REPLENISHED, AND CARED FOR.

The gift of a new day is yours.
Shani T. Night
Use it wisely.

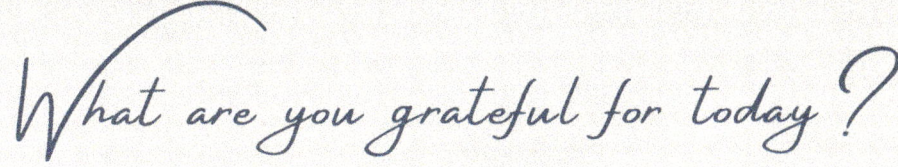

What are you grateful for today?

(Consider gratitude and appreciation for what already exists in your life.)

_____
_____
_____
_____
_____
_____
_____
_____
_____
_____
_____
_____
_____
_____

The gift of hope is yours.
The gift of dreams is yours.
The gift of love is yours.
The gift of ability is yours.
Use it and enjoy!

Shani T. Night

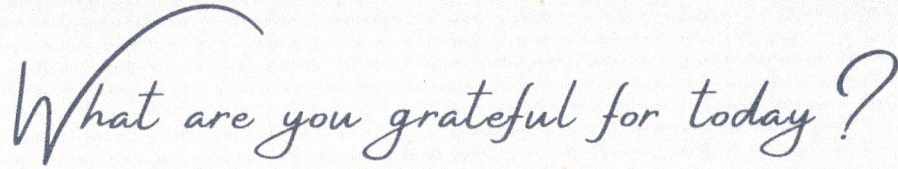

What are you grateful for today?

(Consider gratitude and appreciation for what already exists in your life.
Practice gratitude breathing by taking slow, deep breaths while focusing on what you are thankful for each time you inhale and exhale.)

_____
_____
_____
_____
_____
_____
_____
_____
_____
_____
_____
_____
_____
_____

The sun will rise
and
we will try again.
Every day is a new beginning.

Shani T. Night

New Beginnings

New beginnings refer to starting fresh, opening up new doors and opportunities, and embarking on new journeys. It is a time to let go of the past and embrace change and growth. New beginnings can be exciting and scary, as they often involve leaving one's comfort zone and taking risks. They offer a chance to start over, to pursue dreams and goals that may have been put on hold or abandoned, and to create a better future for oneself. Examples of new beginnings include starting a new job, moving to a new city, starting a new relationship, or even making a significant lifestyle change such as committing to a healthier diet or fitness routine.

Listening

The art of listening is the skill of giving complete attention to what someone is saying or trying to communicate. It involves paying close attention to the words, tone, and body language of the person speaking, as well as putting aside any distractions or preconceptions that may hinder the communication process. Good listeners are patient and empathetic, seeking to truly understand the message being conveyed and responding thoughtfully and respectfully. The art of listening is crucial to effective communication, building relationships, and achieving mutual understanding in both personal and professional settings.

"Life experiences are just that. Learn to enjoy life and take the hits along the way; they help you grow and learn."

Shani T. Night

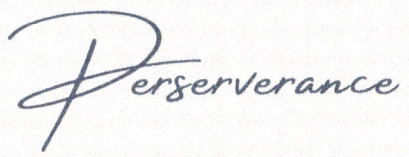

Perserverance

Perseverance refers to the ability to persist in the face of difficulties or challenges. It is the quality of continuing to work towards a goal or objective, even when obstacles or setbacks occur. Perseverance requires determination, patience, and a strong will to overcome adversity. Those who possess perseverance are often able to stay focused on their goals and maintain their motivation, even when progress is slow or difficult.

"Life experiences are just that. They do not define who you are; they help you grow and learn." Shani T. Night

Consistency vs. Perserverance

Consistency and perseverance are both important traits that can help individuals achieve their goals and succeed in various areas of life, but they differ in certain ways.

Consistency refers to the ability to maintain a particular level of performance, behavior, or effort over a period of time. It involves showing up and putting in the work consistently, even when it's difficult or when the results may not be immediate or apparent. Consistency can help individuals build habits, establish routines, and maintain momentum.

Perseverance, on the other hand, refers to the ability to persist in the face of challenges, obstacles, or setbacks. It involves a combination of determination, resilience, and grit. Perseverance can help individuals overcome difficulties and achieve long-term goals by refusing to give up, even when progress is slow or difficult.

In short, consistency involves maintaining a certain level of effort or behavior over time, while perseverance involves continuing to push forward in the face of challenges and obstacles. While both traits are valuable and can contribute to success, they each require different approaches and mindsets.

"Life is not regarded the same because everyone is not treated the same."
-Shan T. Night

We Need More Compassion!
We Need Understanding!
We Need Love!

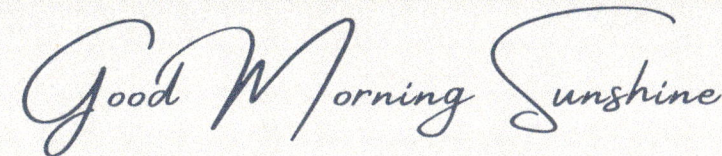

Good Morning Sunshine

(I always welcome sunshine into my day, first thing in the morning: so welcome sunshine and an open heart to declutter your mind. Continue to do this each day. Share thoughts on how you feel about doing this below.)

_____
_____
_____
_____
_____
_____
_____
_____
_____
_____
_____

"Learn to be still in the moment." Shan T. Night

"The goal of life is to be present"
Shan T. Night

Learning to be still in the moment means being present and fully aware of your thoughts, feelings, and surroundings without judgment or distraction. It involves focusing your attention on the present moment, being mindful of your breath and physical sensations, and observing your thoughts and emotions with curiosity and openness. This practice can help you cultivate a greater sense of calm, clarity, and perspective, and reduce stress, anxiety, and negative thoughts. By learning to be still in the moment, you can also develop a deeper connection with yourself and the world around you, and enhance your overall well-being and quality of life.

"Confidence builds
character."

Shani T. Night

Confidence

(Building strong character can help boost self-confidence. When we have a clear sense of our values, beliefs, and principles, we are more likely to make decisions and take actions that align with those qualities. This sense of alignment can lead to a greater sense of self-efficacy and self-assuredness, which can, in turn, build confidence.

Getting a clear sense of one's values, beliefs, and principles requires self-reflection and introspection. Here are some exercises and strategies that may help:

Make a list
Write down the values, beliefs, and principles that come to mind. This can include things like honesty, compassion, fairness, and respect.

Reflect on your past experiences
Consider times when you felt particularly proud or fulfilled. What values, beliefs, or principles were you honoring in those moments?

Consider your priorities
Think about what is most important to you in life. Is it family, career, personal growth, or something else? What values or beliefs are tied to these priorities?

Remember, getting a clear sense of your values, beliefs, and principles is an ongoing process. It's important to regularly check in with yourself and reflect on how you are living in alignment with these core aspects of yourself.

When we act with integrity and are honest and reliable in our interactions with others, we are more likely to be trusted and respected, which can also contribute to greater confidence. So, while confidence and character are distinct concepts, there is certainly an interplay between the two.

Recognize

"Regrets are powerful."
– Shani T. Night
(learn from them
Write down your regrets.)

Embrace Change!

Embracing Change

Embracing change means accepting and adapting to new circumstances and situations, whether they are positive or negative. Change is a natural and inevitable part of life, and resisting it can lead to stress, anxiety, and missed opportunities. Embracing change requires flexibility, openness, and a willingness to learn and grow from new experiences. It also involves letting go of old habits and patterns that may no longer serve us and being open to new possibilities and ways of thinking. By embracing change, we can navigate life's ups and downs with greater ease and resilience and ultimately lead more fulfilling and meaningful lives.

I'm building my foundation on positivity!

Shane T Night

Reflect

(Continue to reflect on what you've learned and how your
negative thoughts impact your life.
Reflect on your positive thoughts and how they impact your
life. For every negative thought you have today and the next,
counter it with a positive affirmation from your previous
exercise or write a new one down.)

_____
_____
_____
_____
_____
_____
_____
_____
_____
_____
_____
_____
_____

THE KEY IS TO CONTINUE TO ENGAGE POSITIVE THOUGHTS.

Make life make
sense.
It's all in Life's
purpose!
Shani T. Night

Life

Making life make sense is hard. It takes time to find your purpose but it is in finding purpose you start to live. You began to live out your life's mission. In this intentional journey remember to be present in life. Be gentle and forgiving with yourself, we all make mistakes. Get intentional with what matters. Your mental health, physical health, emotional health, and spiritual health.

"FOLLOWING INSPIRATION LEAVES ME FREE AND FREE-FLOWING."

Shani T. Night

"INSPIRATION - FIND IT, AND USE IT BECAUSE YOU'LL NEED IT. THE
INSPIRATION THAT IS."
– SHANI T. NIGHT

THE KEY IS TO GET YOU THINKING ABOUT WHAT INSPIRES
YOU.

"WHEN YOU START PUTTING IT TOGETHER, IT'S NICE. FIND THE PIECES THAT FIT AND THE CONNECTIONS WILL START. LIFE WILL START TO CONNECT WITH YOUR DREAMS. YOUR DREAMS WILL START TO CONNECT WITH YOUR MOTIVATION AND INSPIRATION."

- SHANI T. NIGHT

"INSPIRATION - FIND IT, AND USE IT BECAUSE YOU'LL NEED IT. THE INSPIRATION THAT IS."
– SHANI T. NIGHT

THE KEY IS TO GET YOU THINKING ABOUT WHAT INSPIRES YOU.

"*Find the pieces to make it work.*"

SHANI T. NIGHT

"INSPIRATION - FIND IT, AND USE IT BECAUSE YOU'LL NEED IT. THE INSPIRATION THAT IS."
– SHANI T. NIGHT

THE KEY IS TO GET YOU THINKING ABOUT WHAT INSPIRES YOU.

Inspiration

Inspiration is the process of being mentally stimulated to do or feel something, especially something creative. It is a feeling of enthusiasm or motivation that comes from experiencing or witnessing something that is uplifting or thought-provoking. Inspiration can come from a variety of sources, such as nature, art, music, literature, and personal experiences. It can be a powerful force that helps people overcome challenges, pursue their goals and dreams, and live more fulfilling lives.

Reflect

(What inspires you? Reflect on the page on the left and write down your answer as it comes to mind. Also, refer back to Book 1, and see if what you've written relates to your goals and aspirations.)

_____

_____

_____

_____

_____

_____

_____

_____

_____

_____

_____

_____

_____

_____

_____

Intentionally Positive

Positive Quotes

Have fun here.
Enjoy the positive quotes and write down your thoughts. Of course, there's still more to do, but here are a few positive quotes to get you through each day.

"Somehow, the universe will find you to fulfill your part!"

SHANI T. NIGHT

Good Morning Sunshine

(I always welcome sunshine into my day, first thing in the morning.)

"I LOVE INSPIRATION BECAUSE YOU NEVER KNOW WHERE IT WILL LEAD YOU. INSPIRATION IS ALL AROUND.

IT'S LIKE LIGHTNING IN MY SOUL. WHEN IT STRIKES IT'S UNDENIABLE."

- SHANI T. NIGHT

"Inspiration - It feeds my soul and expands my mind
to things I never thought possible."
– Shani T. Night

"Creativity is to be admired, appreciated, and loved."

Shani T. Night

Good Morning Sunshine

(Be creative!)

"FEAR DOESN'T CROSS THE ROAD; THE FEARLESS DO"

– Shani T. Night

Good Morning Sunshine

(Be fearless!)

I don't live suspiciously but I move cautiously. *Shani T. Night*

Good Morning Sunshine

(I always welcome sunshine into my day, first thing in the morning. Don't forget to do this. It's essential.)

"All the different levels of complexity that make up a person matter"

Shani T. Night

Good Morning Sunshine

(I always welcome sunshine into my day, first thing in the morning. Don't forget to do this. It's essential.)

A Good
Day Starts
with
Positivity!

Good Morning Sunshine

(I always welcome sunshine into my day, first thing in the morning. Don't forget to do this. It's essential.)

"IT'S THROUGH ALL THE SOUL SEARCHING, LOVE LOST, AND MISTAKES THAT YOU FIND YOURSELF. YOU DISCOVER YOUR TRUTH AND YOUR STRENGTH.

YOU CAN NOW SOAR."

- Shani J. Night

Good Morning Sunshine

"Know your worth, and then proceed. Know your value, and you will know when to supersede."
- Shani T. Night

"I aspire to be the best part of me."
Shani T. Night

Good Morning Sunshine

(Are you present in your life?)

"There is stress at every turn in life. Learn how to avoid those stresses and not add to them."

Shani T. Night

Time to chase your dreams!

Good Morning Sunshine

(Let go, declutter your mind, and stay positive.)

"I CLIMB ON THE BACKS OF THOSE THAT NEVER GAVE UP."

Shani T. Night

Good Morning Sunshine

(Never give up on being the best person you can be.)

"I AM MY ANCESTORS BEFORE I EVEN KNEW YOU, I REFLECTED YOU, AND I NOW CARRY YOU WITH ME."

Shani T. Night

Good Morning Sunshine

"Chasing your dreams is not whimsical. It's magical."
– Shani T. Night

"People will be people. Do not look for what you want in others. Look for it in yourself. Love, acceptance, support, or whatever it is, give it to yourself first before seeking it elsewhere."

SHANI T. NIGHT

Good Morning Sunshine

(I used this quote to remind myself where my joy comes from and why I alone can give it or take it away. During my journey of realizing my dreams buried deep within from childhood, I remembered that I was looking for others to support me and accept what I was doing. When really, I didn't need that. What I needed was to give it to myself first.)

"We should all insist we show up for ourselves if nothing else."

Shani T. Night

Good Morning Sunshine

(This quote came from the previous quote. Once I realized that I needed to show up for myself first, the rest became easy. Not just in dreams and goals but in self-care. We show up for everyone else. Why not start with ourselves.)

"My greatest successes have come from where I least expected them."

Shani T. Night

Identify your greatest successes

(Recognize and appreciate what you least expected)

"It is through mistakes, you find yourself. Your true self."

SHANI T. NIGHT

Identify your mistakes

(You don't want to make them again)

"Your decisions are your own, and the consequences are uniquely yours."

SHANI T. NIGHT

Identify a decision you made

(and its consequence (good or bad))

"Push through the pain of the past and into the happiness of the future."

SHANI T. NIGHT

Deal

I wrote the quote on the left while dealing with my pain from the past. As a Pentagon contractor, I was there on 911, and it took years for me to really deal with the pain of that day. Learn from pain and push through into the happiness of the future - Shani T. Night.)

Write your thoughts on what you are dealing with or have dealt with in the past or present.

"Be fearless and life will be limitless. You'll inspire someone along the way."
— Shani T. Night

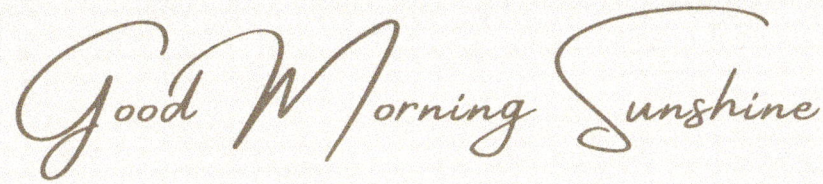

Good Morning Sunshine

(I used to be fearless until one day, my shield was gone. I can recall the moment I started caring what others thought about me. It was a message delivered by someone I thought was a friend. "I've learned that being fearless is a shield that allowed me to be me and that my shield will scare some, but it will allow others to be fearless.
- Shani T. Night)

Are you fearless? What's your shield?

"WALKING IN YOUR TRUTH IS BRAVE, AND SHINING IN YOUR PURPOSE IS DIVINE."

Shani T. Night

Good Morning Sunshine

(Learn to walk in your truth and address anything that takes you away from it. This one is hard. Work on it every chance you get.)

"Do not lead with anger. Lead with truth, love, and peace."

Shani T. Night

Good Morning Sunshine

(Learn to walk in your truth and address anything that takes you away from it. This one is hard. Work on it every chance you get.)

OPERATE FROM LOVE.

Shani T. Night

Good Morning Sunshine

(Learn to walk in your truth and address anything that takes you away from it. This one is hard. Work on it every chance you get.)

Good Morning Sunshine

(Learn to walk in your truth and address anything that takes you away from it. This one is hard. Work on it every chance you get.)

Recognize

"Regrets are powerful." – Shani T. Night
(learn from them - write down your regrets.)

Bloom where you are.
You are built for self-improvement,
so improve. Fix what you need to
have healthy soil (foundation). If
the soil is bad, improve it. Treat it
with care and prevent contamination.
Become wiser, so next season you know
what you need to do to cleanse your
soil (soul).

Shani T. Night

Positive Thoughts

"STRESS IS THE CONDUCTOR ON A BAD DAY, AND PEACE IS THE CONDUCTOR ON A GOOD DAY."

Shani T Night

Positive Thoughts

"I am different from yesterday.
I will be different tomorrow.
I am evolving and growing.
I am using every moment of this life to do so."

Shani T Night

Positive Thoughts

There is nothing
you can't do.

Shani J. Night

Positive Thoughts

Facts

"I can walk away
from anything and
anyone.
Self- preservation
is a must."

Shani T Night

Positive Thoughts

Removing Fear from my Vocabulary!

Positive Thoughts

The fear of failing will stop you from achieving!

Positive Thoughts

Feelings are like waves, just figure out which one to catch.

Shani T Night

Positive Thoughts

"I am making room for whom
I am meant to be."

Shani T. Night

Positive Thoughts

"Making time for me feels good."

Shani T. Night

Positive Thoughts

"Making room for who I am to become." *Shani T. Night*

Positive Thoughts

"All the possibilities of life are within you."

-Shan T. Night

Positive Thoughts

"Set no limitations and live."

Shani T. Night

Positive Thoughts

Positive Thoughts

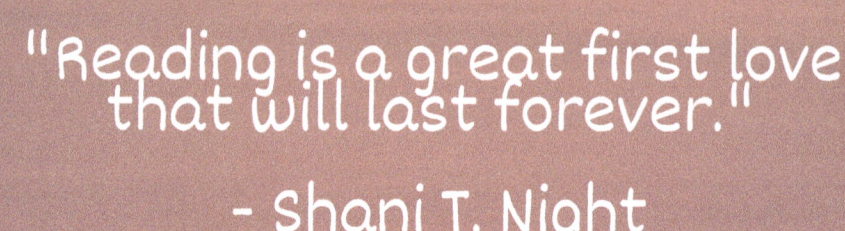

"Reading is a great first love
that will last forever."

- Shani T. Night

Positive Thoughts

TODAY WE DREAM, TOMORROW WE INSPIRE.

SHANI T. NIGHT

Positive Thoughts

Intentionally Positive

Poems

Positive Thoughts

WE ARE AN ORCHESTRATOR OF
PROJECTS
A BALANCER OF PEOPLE
A WEARER OF MANY HATS

WE ARE THE CALM IN THE MIDDLE OF
CHAOS
WE ARE MOMS
WE ARE WOMEN
WE ARE PROJECT MANAGERS
WE ARE HUMAN

WRITTEN BY SHANI T. NIGHT
(IN ORDER TO DEAL WITH THE DAY TO
DAY CHAOS OF LIFE)

Positive Thoughts

WE HAVE LOST SO MANY SOULS.
TOO MANY IN THE ENUMERATION OF
OUR ROLES
IN THE ROLES, WE PLAY
DO WE DARE TO SAY

IN THE GRIPS OF OUR TWENTIES,
WE REVELLED IN THE WAR OF
LOSTNESS,
SOARED IN THE MOMENTS OF
GREATNESS
SOURED IN THE IMMENSE
SUFFOCATION OF LONELINESS

LOSS CONTINUES
AS LIFE CONTINUES
AND EACH YEAR, WE BLOOM
TAKING WITH US THE UNBLOOMED
SOULS OF OUR PAST.

WRITTEN BY SHANI T. NIGHT
(IN ORDER TO DEAL WITH LOSS)

Positive Thoughts

BUILDING BOXES UPON BOXES.
DO I FIGURE OUT WHO THE FOX IS?

STORING PAIN UPON PAIN.
CAN I STOP THE RAIN?

IN THE LIGHT OF DAY WILL I BE
OKAY?

IN THE DARK OF NIGHT WILL I BE
JUST AND RIGHT?

IN THE SHADOW WILL I BE IN FLIGHT
OR IN THE LIGHT WILL I STAND AND
FIGHT?

THE SIDE YOU CHOOSE RESTS UPON
YOU.

WRITTEN BY SHANI T. NIGHT
(DISCOVERING LIFE)

Positive Thoughts

"I SMILE BECAUSE I KNOW THE KEYS TO LIFE ARE LOVE AND KINDNESS.

I SMILE BECAUSE IT GIVES ME PEACE.

I SMILE BECAUSE I HAVE A LOVE FROM WITHIN.

I SMILE BECAUSE THERE IS NO GREATER PLEASURE THAN A WIN.

I SMILE BECAUSE YOU CAN NEVER TELL ANYTHING OTHER THAN."

WRITTEN BY SHANI T. NIGHT (DISCOVERING LOVE OF SELF)

Positive Thoughts

"I AM
INSPIRATION
FLOWING IN THE
WIND.
I AM STRENGTH
GROWING FROM
WITHIN.

I AM LOVE ON THE
MOVE.
I AM ALL THAT I
AM BECAUSE OF
YOU."

Shani T. Night

Positive Thoughts

I intentionally did a house cleaning and redesigned my personal space to allow more light and openness for positivity and happiness.

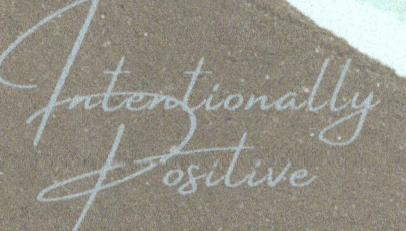

I intentionally walk almost every morning to destress and give my body what it needs to stay healthy.
More importantly, a brisk walk allows me to clear my mind.
During the COVID pandemic, I realized my body needed more than what I was giving it. It was slow at first, but it has paid off—
Mind, Body, and Spirit.

About the Author

My mission as a certified Happiness Life Wellness Coach is to help individuals live their happiest, healthiest, and most fulfilling lives. I believe that true happiness comes from within, and that by making positive changes in our thoughts, behaviors, and lifestyle, we can transform our lives and achieve lasting well-being.

I am committed to providing personalized coaching that is tailored to the unique needs and goals of each individual client. I believe that everyone has the potential to be happy and successful, and that my role is to provide guidance, support, and encouragement as my clients work to achieve their dreams.

I believe that wellness is a holistic concept that encompasses physical, emotional, and spiritual health, and that by addressing all aspects of wellness, we can achieve a more balanced and fulfilling life. Through my coaching, I aim to empower my clients to take control of their well-being and to make positive changes that will last a lifetime.

My goal is to create a safe, supportive, and non-judgmental space where my clients can explore their thoughts and feelings, overcome their challenges, and discover their true potential. I am passionate about helping others live their best lives, and I am dedicated to making a positive difference in the world, one client at a time.

WWW.SHANITNIGHT.COM

From the Author

"Love yourself through the pain and the letdowns. Like all that you do and how you do it. Try to grow and get better each day. #iamwriting to share what I love most."

— Shani T. Night

" Live out loud,
Live to inspire the next
generation. "

— Shani J. Night

Let's take stock of where you are today.....

Today you are thinking positively. You are a positive thinker. You can see both sides of things, negative and positive, and you choose to be positive.

You are more aware of yourself and your thoughts. But, more importantly, you are true to who you are and whom you want to be.

You are fearless. You don't fear changes or ups and downs.

You surround yourself with positive people.

You don't let mistakes stand in your way.

You are not easily discouraged.

You are your inspiration.

You engage positively.

You are present.

You are happy.   You are

Intentionally Positive

Important Dates

DATE	EVENT	NOTES

Important Dates

DATE	EVENT	NOTES

Take a little time to enjoy the view.

Shani Night

Next Steps

Don't forget to check out the following:
- Intentionally Positive Path to Positive Change: A Guided Journal for Transformation Vol. I
- Intentionally Positive planner: Positive Quotes, Affirmations, and Poems for daily life inspiration
- Free session with the purchase of this book **(schedule on my website)**

Intentionally Positive Journals and Planners are sold on my website:
www.shanitnight.com

www.ingramcontent.com/pod-product-compliance
Lightning Source LLC
Chambersburg PA
CBHW051624120626
46551CB00014B/1923